SNOWFALL 2013

TOGETHER WE FACED IT ALL

Concept: Nicola Green

Managing editor: Miles Cowsill

Writer: Trevor Barrett

Designer: Ian Smith

Photographs: as individually credited

Front cover: Paul Marriott (www.paulmarriottphotography.com)

Rear cover: Rachel Bridges

lilypublications.co.uk

First published in the
Isle of Man in 2013 by
Lily Publications Ltd
PO Box 33
Ramsey
Isle of Man IM99 4LP

Jurby Church.

Miles Cowsill

2

CONTENTS

ACKNOWLEDGEMENTS

Lily Publications would like to express sincere thanks to the following for helping to make this project a success:

John Lewis – Gomer Press Ltd
Lexicon Bookshop
Bridge Bookshop
St Paul's Bookshop
Pat Leatherbarrow
Manx Independent Carriers
Manx Radio
Paul Marriott Photography
Paul Moulton – MTTV
Ronaldsway Meteorological Office
All the people who have visited our Facebook page and sent in photographs.

FOREWORD

The Isle of Man Agricultural Benevolent Trust (IOMABT) is grateful to Lily Publications for compiling this collection of photographs taken during and after the big snow event of March 2013, and for donating a portion of the book's net profit to assist us in our work. A small autonomous Isle of Man charity (no. 72111c) founded in 1995, we respond to genuine cases of hardship in the agricultural and associated sectors.

Potential beneficiaries can self-refer or may be brought to the attention of the Trust officers by third parties. All funds raised on behalf of the ABT, or from donations, stay on the island, and as the Trust is run by volunteers there are no administrative costs.

All referrals are dealt with in the strictest confidence, and when assessing need the Trust's small management committee has a very good track record of discretion and professionalism. Indeed, most of the members have been with the Trust from the start, including legal adviser Will Kelly and financial adviser Charles Fargher. Long-standing immediate past chairman Peter Kennaugh retired in 2012 after 17 years on the committee.

To date, financial assistance has been granted in cases of accident, illness and genuine hardship. This support can take the form of one-off grants or interest-free loans, and each case is assessed individually by the Trust's advisers, who then make their recommendation to the directors. However, where there is a need, and issues such as welfare are concerned, the Trust acts very swiftly.

The Trust is extremely grateful to all those individuals and organisations who have supported us in the past, or have expressed a wish to do so in various ways in response to the extreme weather of 22nd and 23rd March 2013. The Trust's policy of not acting in commercially-challenging circumstances has been set aside in the light of the amazing public response to the losses incurred by some farmers, and monies have been raised and donated to the Trust specifically for the purpose of assisting these cases. The blizzard and drift conditions, particularly in the central hills and down the west of the island from Michael to Ronague, have left many thousands of sheep, cattle and poultry dead.

Prior to the March snow, our island's farmers had already suffered

Wayne Smith

10 months of appalling weather which ruined many harvests and, going into winter, produced sileage and hay crops of very low quality. The waterlogged ground meant that most green crops sown for winter feed were a disaster, as were many of the vegetables. Everyone was hopeful that a good spring would offer some relief, but sadly the reverse happened, the Big Snow making it the worst in living memory – hardly the springboard to a rewarding and satisfying 2013.

The industry's elder statesmen have recalled the extreme weather events of 1947 and 1963, but where those differ from March's Big Snow is that they occurred in winter and had long gone come the following spring.

The Trust's thanks go to Miles and his team at Lily Publications for their efforts in bringing together this brilliant collection of photographs, recording for posterity the snow event of March 2013, and to all those people who have assisted in its production and provided their services at cost – and of course to the photographers for capturing the images.

To be considered for assistance from the Trust, either personally or on behalf of others who may need support, please contact Trust secretary Jonathan Corlett by telephone on **07624 410154** or email *jonathan.corlett@manx.net*

To donate to the IOMABT please send a cheque, made payable to IOM Agricultural Benevolent Trust, c/o Mr Charles Fargher at Ballafreer House, Union Mills, IM4 4AB, or by using the PayPal link on the Trust's Facebook status.

Graham Crowe, Chairman,
Isle of Man Agricultural Benevolent Trust
April 2013

CODE RED

Throughout the week beginning Monday 18th March 2013, weather forecasters at the Isle of Man's airport-based Ronaldsway Meteorological Office at Ballasalla paid very close attention to the computer model predictions.

By Thursday 21st March all signs pointed to a serious event. At 09.30 the duty forecaster duly issued a Code Red weather warning: significant snowfall overnight, continuing during Friday and into Saturday, the snow accumulating down to sea level in some western areas. With the snow would come gale-force or severe gale-force east to south-east winds gusting at up to 60 mph and producing snow drifts.

As early as 3 o'clock the next morning, Friday 22nd, staff of the Manx Electricity Authority were battling to reach up to a thousand customers in the west and north to restore supply, the combination of heavy snow and arctic winds having toppled trees and power lines. Their task wasn't helped by the deep drifts formed against fences, hedges and walls, making roads impassable, particularly to remoter properties and communities.

Friday also saw schools closing early and ferry services severely disrupted. A consequence of the latter was that Co-Operative Food, looking at the bigger picture and the severity of the weather, chose to charter a Royal Air Force Hercules transporter to fly in 18 tonnes of food and provisions for re-stocking its 10 stores across the island.

Code Red was already living up to its rating and threat – and with a vengeance.

'Smile – we're on camera!'

Michael Brown

DIGGING DEEP

As the severe weather rapidly tightened its grip, Ronaldsway's Met Office records revealed that it was the worst snow for 50 years.

Not since Britain's infamous Big Freeze of 1963 had the island been hit so hard, and those to bear the brunt this time around would be livestock farmers in the west and north whose animals were out in the hills and at the mercy of the elements – and especially the deep drifts.

Cattle, less vulnerable than sheep, are better able to survive such trauma but lambs are at much higher risk. To make matters worse, many farmers had moved their animals from the barns to the fields earlier than they normally would because food supplies were low, the wet weather of summer 2012 having produced a poor yield. There was another worry too: this is the time of year when many cows and sheep give birth.

With so much of the high ground in the west and north covered by the drifts, the task of digging for surviving animals would be gruelling, and heavy losses inevitable.

Over the weekend of the 23rd and 24th March, sheep farmer Robbie Christian, who grazes his 1,000-strong flock on the hills between Kirk Michael and Bareegarrow, dug out just 100 survivors from drifts that were 10 feet deep. "Even if you can find them, digging them out is nigh on impossible. Sheep just go with the wind and when they find a wall they huddle together and suffocate. It's a disaster."

Much of his flock was heavily pregnant and lambing was due to begin in mid April. "Even sheep which survive will struggle to produce milk," he feared.

And there was little comfort from the Met Office, who said that although the worst of the snow should be over by Tuesday (26th March), temperatures would remain very low, ruling out any prospect of a quick thaw.

At Corvalley, close to Peel, farmer Trevor Quirk lost many cattle and sheep. Although he'd rescued 45 sheep, 65 were still missing and of those he rescued many were later put down by a vet. A dozen cattle died too when the weight of snow on the shed roof caused part of it to collapse. He couldn't get in to feed them and the water froze, but

the remaining 90 cows were freed by digger.

Another story of loss was that of farmer Angela Kelly of Rhencullen, Kirk Michael. Half of her livestock died when the roofs of two steel sheds collapsed on top of them. It was a cruel twist of fate, as she'd moved them into the sheds to shelter from the freezing conditions, but the weight of 5-6 feet of snow proved too much for the roofs to bear. The family also lost cows, calves, sheep and lambs, and many sheep that survived were subsequently put down by a vet. But two bulls fared rather better, firemen risking their lives to pull them out.

On Greeba mountain, farmer Helen Kermode of Hilltop Rise said that her surviving stock owed their lives to about 40 volunteers who battled to reach her land on Tuesday 26th armed with sledges and shovels. Drifts of up to 15 feet were making many of her fields inaccessible, and on Wednesday 27th she had to call the Fire and Rescue Service to get drinking water for a bull stuck in a barn. "It's been horrendous – I've never seen conditions like it."

As the scale of such difficulties faced by the island's livestock farmers became apparent, many appeals for help were made through Facebook and other means, and the response from the Manx community was overwhelming. Teams of qualified volunteers worked all hours digging for livestock, carrying feed across land inaccesible to tractors and moving surviving animals to safer ground. But Ray Craine, president of the Manx National Farmers Union, was quick to warn people not to attempt accessing the mountain areas to look for livestock unless they were members of a supervised rescue. "In this weather the hills are dangerous places – many gullies and drops are hidden by snow and we don't want a sheep hunt turning into a manhunt."

He also pointed out that lowland farmers had been less affected by the weather, and those not tied up by lambing and calving were better able to use their specialised skills, knowledge and equipment to help their fellow farmers.

Onchan resident Savina Thomas took a day off to help and

Andrea Lace

described the community's response as fantastic. "There were people I'd never met before, and of all ages, struggling to get through the fields and really wanting to help. Some of the sheep we pulled out alive had been down there for four days and were buried in five feet of snow. It was great to see them alive."

Volunteer Sara Nolan went one further, taking an orphaned lamb home to bottle feed it every couple of hours. "Snowy the lamb is now tucked up in a dog bed with a hot water bottle and towels."

One of the more novel and enterprising ideas to find sheep buried in snow drifts was to enlist the help of an unmanned helicopter equipped with a thermal imaging camera to detect body heat. The flaw in this ingenious idea was that any animals trapped would have been there too long to be giving off sufficient heat. Nevertheless, before returning to its intended employment – taking aerial photographs for land and building surveys – the camera managed to find a few sheep on the hills above the Gooseneck overlooking Ramsey.

Chief Minister Alan Bell said he was heartened by the way the community had rallied round. And Agriculture Minister Phil Gawne MHK added: "The Manx public have really stepped up to the plate and delivered amazing support to the agricultural community and to neighbours generally. And I'm pleased to announce that the Council of Ministers supports the idea of initiating an emergency fund to help farmers at this very difficult time – the worst that many of them have ever known. In addition, payments applicable under the countryside care scheme are being brought forward from April and the vast majority of farmers will receive them this week. And the charge for disposing of dead animals will be waived."

On the same theme, the Isle of Man Agricultural Benevolent Trust, which responds to hardship in the industry, received a £15,000 boost courtesy of the Isle of Man Young Farmers, and newly-formed Manx trio Barrule was encouraging fans to download a song for free and make a donation. The trio recorded the 18th-century Manx ballad *Ny Kirree fo Niaghtey* (*The Sheep Under the Snow*) on their debut album, a percentage of the CD sales going to the Trust too.

Rescue of an elderly resident from her farm in Cronk-y-Voddy.

Andrea Lace

ALL PART OF THE SERVICE

When the Code Red storm struck it was to prove a severe test – not only for beleaguered farmers but also for many of those working in public services.

As the arctic blizzards and gale-force winds gusting to more than 60 mph brought down trees and power lines in the west and north of the island, emergency teams knew that it would be a matter of days rather than hours before they could reach areas worst hit by snow drifts up to 16 feet deep.

Amongst the busiest – if not the front line – were the linesmen of the Manx Electricity Authority. The remotest areas, in desperate need of their help, were inaccessible by vehicle, so there was no alternative but to battle through snow that was waist deep. Working on a round-the-clock shift basis, the MEA team comprised around 50 field staff and 40 support staff.

The priority was to restore power to the most vulnerable – but the longer the power was down the greater the number of vulnerable people grew, developing into a severe test of patience and understanding all round. And with power lines in some areas suffering significant damage, notably Ballaugh Curraghs, Cronk-y-Voddy, Dalby and parts of Abbeylands, there was no quick fix. Even the emergency services resorted to heavy plant to respond as quickly as possible to those in need of urgent help.

Teams from the island's Department of Infrastructure worked until dark to reach stranded areas, finally making it to Cronk-y-Voddy on 24th March and enabling MEA staff to begin restoring power there.

Although no phone lines were damaged or affected by the extreme weather, Manx Telecom staff spent several hectic days fighting to maintain services. In some areas where power was down or temporary electricity supplies were employed, network problems and reduced mobile coverage were experienced. And in the few instances when batteries were exhausted, lack of access meant that generators couldn't be provided. Manx Telecom's helpdesk was inundated, receiving 500 more calls than the average and a further 300 calls to the emergency services.

Coastguard teams too were called into action to help evacuate a mother and baby from their powerless home, which was surrounded

Debbie Sanderson

13

by heavy snow drifts, at Cronk-y-Voddy crossroads (approximately midway between Peel and Kirk Michael on the A3). The team from Ramsey, approaching from the north, could get no further than Kirk Michael. Fortunately, the Peel coastguard team had better luck, reaching them from the Ballacraine crossroads by following an excavator which by chance was clearing the road ahead. But the last quarter of a mile had to be on foot. Mother and baby were then walked to a coastguard 4x4 which took them to Noble's Hospital.

And some homes received emergency medical supplies delivered by quad bike.

On a sporting note, Highways Director Richard Pearson promised that the TT course would be ready for racing despite the appalling weather and the problems experienced in 2010 and 2011, when water in surface cracks froze and caused severe damage.

Firefighters from Kirk Michael put in sterling service too as an eventful few days saw them rescuing motorists stuck in the snow at Rhencullen/Bishopscourt – though to reach them it took a 6-wheel-drive vehicle to battle through 4-foot drifts. "I've never seen conditions like it," said Station Officer John Cashin. "It was really incredible."

The firefighters dropped the rescued motorists back at their homes and checked whether they had power, as 200-300 homes in the village were without. And in their efforts and determination to help the community, they pooled their local knowledge, making a list of the people they knew in the areas most affected, such as Ballameanaugh, Cronk Aashen and Cronk-y-Voddy. But on Saturday their efforts were hampered by the sheer volume of snow, and just a mile and a half out of the village they were faced with a 15-foot drift and set about delivering fuel and groceries to homes on foot. They also worked with the ambulance service, rescuing people with medical conditions from their homes. And firefighters helped to rescue 40 sheep buried under 15 feet of snow at Upper Ballacooley in Kirk Michael.

Infrastructure Minister David Cretney said that the cost of clearing up could exceed the department's budget – but he praised staff working 12-hour shifts to re-open roads hit by snow drifts and MEA staff who'd restored power to hundreds of homes.

"It's been a massive team effort," he said. "All those involved in my department, the MEA, police, coastguard, private contractors and volunteers across the island – they're all heroes."

Manx Electricity Authority Chief Executive Phil King praised the flexibility and ingenuity of the staff and those engineers having to face extreme conditions. "It's been a complete team job. Communication and prioritising has been the key to the whole task. Even staff who normally work in IT have been out as runners to take food to the

Opposite: MEA field staff worked on a round-the-clock basis to reinstate power lines.

Wind and snow 'art',
Snaefell Summit Hotel.

Ralph Jackson

engineers. And even Ramsey Power Station – usually unmanned – was manned around the clock."

Chief Minister Alan Bell also paid tribute to the "truly heroic response" of public service staff in clearing roads, restoring power and saving livestock.

"The dedication shown by people in the public services has been hugely impressive," he said. "The weather has been exceptional – but so have they, and they deserve the praise and thanks of the entire island. The worst snow storm for half a century has disrupted lives and damaged livelihoods in country areas. Yet it's very reassuring to see that in the face of extreme adversity the Isle of Man retains such a strong community spirit and dedication to public service."

Andrea Lace

Kirk Michael, Saturday 23rd March.

Glacial sculpture.

Andrea Lace

An undercover police operation?

Andrea Lace

Cronk-y-Voddy.

Little London 1

Andrea Lace

Andrea Lace

Andrea Lace

Andrea Lace

Andrea Lace

Andrea Lace

Looking for sheep, North Barrule, overlooking Ramsey (Tuesday 26th).

Andy Kerruish

Love is all around!

Annie Lowey

A view from near the Albert Tower, Ramsey.

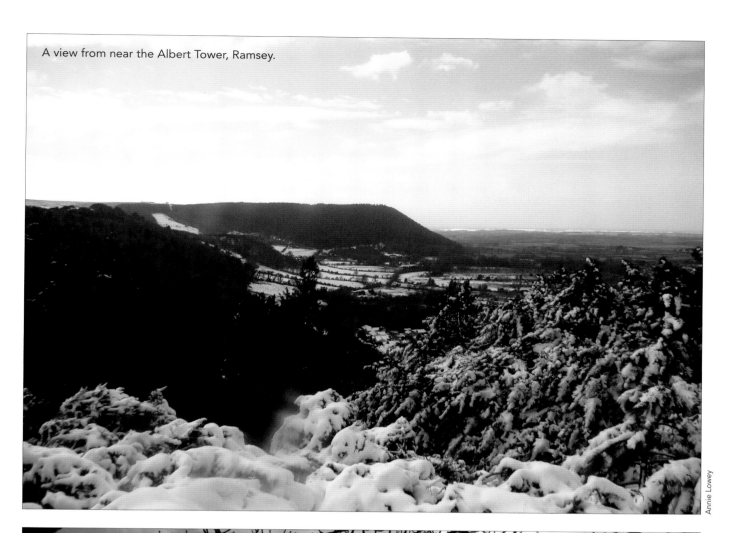

Annie Lowey

North Barrule.

Annie Lowey

Ballamoar Farm, Ballaugh: Aaron Curphey and daughter Isla digging sheep out 6 days after the snow began with mum, Cheryl, below.

Cheryl Curphey

Cheryl Curphey

Glen Helen.

Making friends with a snowman.

Ballanass.

Hope, from the railway.

Debbie Sanderson

Easter egg hunt.

Debbie Sanderson

Mullein.

Debbie Sanderson

Railway line: no trains today!

Debbie Sanderson

Chris Darnill

'Am I in Australia yet?'

Making tracks...

Debbie Sanderson

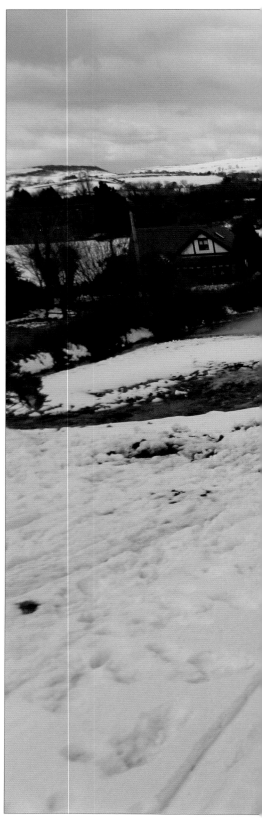

Debbie Sanderson

A Douglas tram horse in Patrick Road, St John's.

Whitehouse, Kirk Michael.

Gordon Moore

Glen Wyllin.

Gordon Moore

Gordon Moore

Cooper's Close, Kirk Michael.

Gordon Moore

24 Hour Call Out 7 days a week
365 Days a year
Tel: 496259

Oops!

Graham Jones

ROAD CLOSED

Snow through road.

Graham Jones

Ballaugh village.

Ballaugh store.

Graham Jones

Graham Jones

Beach buggy for sale – cool!

Graham Jones

MOUNTAIN VIEW

Graham Jones

Graham Jones

Graham Jones

Graham Jones

Graham Jones

Kirk Michael, Saturday 23rd March.

Ila Griffiths

Ila Griffiths

Jenni Kneale

Arctic ice? No – Ronague.

Cronk ny Arrey Laa (from the Round Table).

Jenni Kneale

This page and following two:
Rescue work – not always successful.

Community spirit.

Rescued sheep.

Ronague down to Cringle Reservoir.

Sleiau Ray from Greeba.

Top of the lane to Scard and Lamode, Sloc Road.

Jenni Kneale

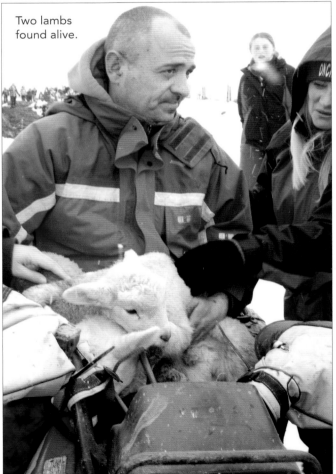

Two lambs found alive.

Jenni Kneale

Jennie Thompson

Ballaugh, looking towards Bride Church.

Jenny Harrison

John Hunter

Jenny Harrison

John Hunter

Jenny Harrison

John Hunter

Jenny Harrison

Top left to bottom left:

Ballacrye Road: Ballaugh Church in the distance.
Ballaugh hills from Ballacrye Road.
All roads lead to more snow.
Glen Mona looking towards Maughold.

Top right to bottom right:

11th Milestone.
Burnside, Cronk-y-Voddy.
Snow place like home?

Cronk-y-Voddy.

John Hunter

Cronk-y-Voddy.

John Hunter

Returning with provisions.

Resting after a hard day's digging.

Throwing snowballs.

All taken from the A4 Peel to Kirk Michael coast road.

In-depth investigation? Cronk-y-Voddy.

Karen Devereau

Two-year-old Kain Devereau helping to find sheep.

Karen Devereau

Braaid.

Braaid.

Braaid.

Douglas.

Mount Rule.

Mount Rule.

Mount Rule.

Sheep rescue.

Michael Brown

Michael Brown

Michael Brown

This page and opposite:
Handley's Corner.

Michael Brown

This page and opposite:
Handley's Corner.

"This snow is driving me quackers!"

Safe at last.

Mike Stephens

Dhoon Church.

Susan Quilliam

Tristan Speight looking after an orphaned lamb rescued by Susan Quilliam from Mount Karrin on 27th March.

Paul Marriott

Moor Cottage, Handley's Corner, Kirk
Michael photographed by 7-year-old
Jack Collier on 23rd March.

Station Road, Ballaugh
photographed by 7-year-old
Jack Collier on 23rd March.

"Although the roads had been cleared enough to get around most of my delivery area within the village, it was very hard work climbing over, under and around the huge drifts that blocked driveways and paths to the houses!"
Peter Maggs, postman

Peter Maggs

Peter Maggs

Peter McEvoy

No trams today – Snaefell Mountain Railway.

Norman Dowd

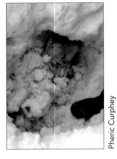

Sunday 24th March, around St Mark's.

Rachel Bridges

Rachel Bridges

Rachel Bridges

Rachel Bridges

Sunrise near Conrhenny Plantation 10 days after first snowfall.

Stuart William

Sue Sanders

Sue Sanders

Sue Sanders

Sue Sanders

Sue Sanders

Sue Sanders

Scenes around Ballalough, West Baldwin.

Antarctic expedition?

Barry Edwards

Barry Edwards

East Baldwin.

Dave Callister

Roller skating?

Ian Pilbeam

Ian Pilbeam

Ian Pilbeam

No way through.

Ian Pilbeam

Colin Russell

Jonathan Crossley

A4 Peel to Kirk Michael.

Jonathan Crossley

Jonathan Crossley

Jonathan Crossley

Lee Partington

Millennium Way between St. Luke's and Beinn Y Phott.

"I'll sleep anywhere."

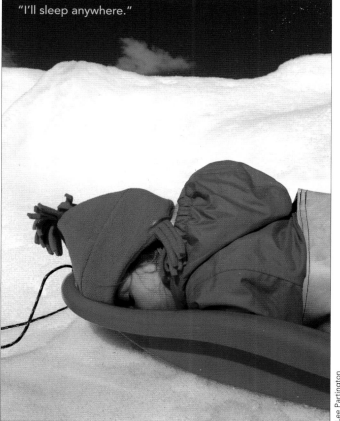

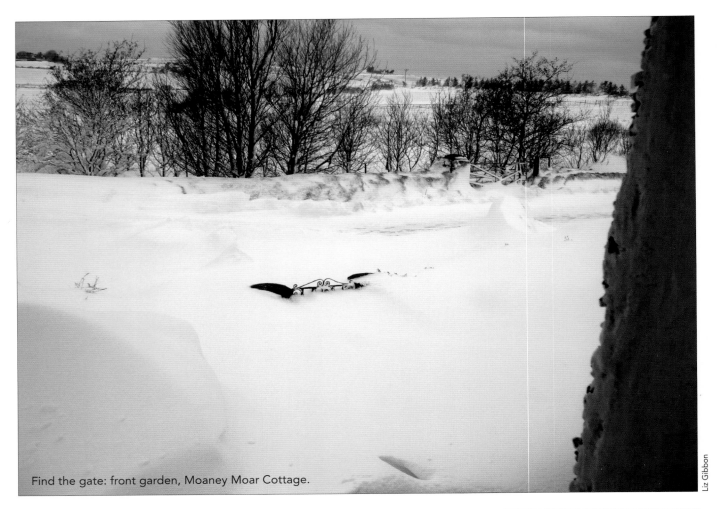

Find the gate: front garden, Moaney Moar Cottage.

Liz Gibbon

On top of the world at the Marshall's post, Cronk-y-Voddy.

Liz Gibbon

Pages 81-83:
Down but not out. MEA at work restoring power lines which have fallen foul of the weather.

MEA

MEA

MEA

MEA

MEA

MEA

MEA

MEA

MEA

MEA

St Peter's clock tower, Peel, framed by a snowy arch.

Patricia Tutt

84

Who needs curtains in this weather?

View towards Market Street, Peel, as the snow clears.

Patricia Tutt

Above Agneash.

Cronk-y-Voddy.

Above Agneash.

Agneash.

Cronk-y-Voddy.

Snaefell summit.

Ralph Jackson

The Bungalow.

Ralph Jackson

Picnic area, Snaefell Summit Hotel.

Ralph Jackson

Ralph Jackson

Snaefell Summit Hotel.

Ralph Jackson

The Bungalow.

Ralph Jackson

Near Glen Moar.

Swiss House, Glen Helen.

Behind Glen Helen Inn.

Fountain, Glen Helen.

Near Gordon.

Top Path, Glen Maye.

Glen Rushen, Glen Maye.

The snow attracts extraterrestrial visitors.

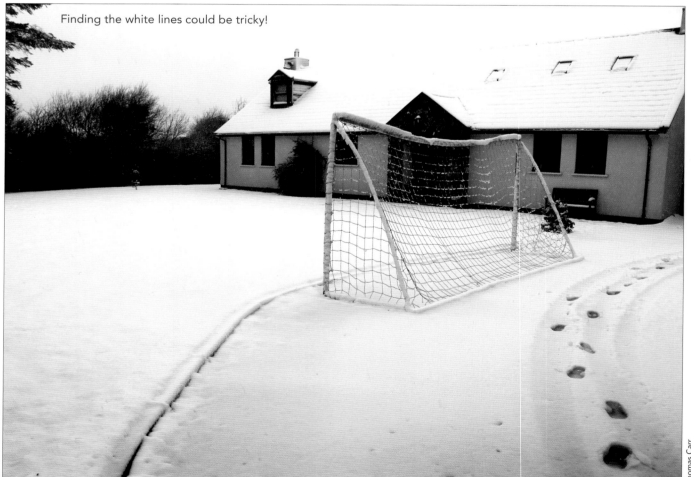

Finding the white lines could be tricky!

Falling flakes.

Frozen roots.

Fun for all! Peel Headlands.

Tony Faragher

Gibb Lane, Peel.

Tony Faragher

House of Manannan, Peel.

Tony Faragher

Peel Castle besieged by snow.

Tony Faragher

Make mine
a snowball!

Tony Faragher

Peel Headlands.

Tony Faragher

Sledging on Peel Headlands.

Tony Faragher

The big clear-up! Peveril Road, Peel.

Tony Faragher

Kirk Michael – Post Office and Pharmacy.

Kirsten Harrison

Looking for sheep, Baltic Road.

Kirsten Harrison

Loaghtan sheep, Whitehouse Farm, Kirk Michael.

Kirsten Harrison